The Unexpected Man

Yasmina Reza's first play, *Conversations après un Enterrement*, won her the Best Author Molière Award and the New Writer Award from the SACD in 1987. Her work for theatre and cinema includes *La Traversée de L'Hiver*, *'Art'*, which received the Molière Award for best play, best production and best author and the *Evening Standard* Award and the Olivier Award for Best Comedy of the Year, a prize-winning adaptation of Steven Berkoff's version of Kafka's *Metamorphose*, and the screenplays *Jascha*, *Jim Mode Ne Pour Aider* and *A Demain*.

Christopher Hampton was born in the Azores in 1946. He wrote his first play, *When Did You Last See My Mother?*, at the age of eighteen. His work for the theatre, television and cinema includes *The Philanthropist*, adaptations from Ibsen and Molière and the screenplays *Dangerous Liaisons*, *Carrington* and *The Secret Agent*, the last two of which he also directed.

by Yasmina Reza
'ART'
translated by Christopher Hampton

also by Christopher Hampton
THE PHILANTHROPIST
TOTAL ECLIPSE
SAVAGES
TREATS
ABLE'S WILL: A PLAY FOR TELEVISION
TALES FROM HOLLYWOOD
LES LIAISONS DANGEREUSES
WHITE CHAMELEON
CHRISTOPHER HAMPTON: PLAYS ONE
(Total Eclipse, The Philanthropist, Savages, Treats)

adaptations
George Steiner's
THE PORTAGE TO SAN CRISTOBAL OF A.H.
Lewis Carroll's
ALICE'S ADVENTURES UNDER GROUND

screenplays
DANGEROUS LIAISONS
THE GINGER TREE
CARRINGTON
TOTAL ECLIPSE
THE SECRET AGENT/NOSTROMO

translations
Odön von Horváth's
TALES FROM THE VIENNA WOODS
Odön von Horváth's
DON JUAN COMES BACK FROM THE WAR
Odön von Horváth's
FAITH, HOPE AND CHARITY
Ibsen's
THE WILD DUCK
Ibsen's
HEDDA GABLER AND A DOLL'S HOUSE
Ibsen's
AN ENEMY OF THE PEOPLE
Molière's
TARTUFFE

YASMINA REZA

The Unexpected Man

translated by
Christopher Hampton

faber and faber
LONDON · BOSTON

First published in 1998
by Faber and Faber Limited
3 Queen Square London WCIN 3AU

Typeset by Faber and Faber Ltd
Printed in England by Mackays of Chatham plc, Chatham, Kent

A CIP record for this book
is available from the British Library

ISBN 0–571–19604–7

4 6 8 10 9 7 5 3

Characters

The Man
The Woman

A train compartment.
A man and a woman.
Nothing realistic. Air. Space.

A deliberate absence of stage directions.
Similarly (except at the end) the necessary silences and
pauses are not indicated in the text.

Each of them self-contained.

The British première of **The Unexpected Man** was performed by the Royal Shakespeare Company at The Pit on 8 April 1998. The cast was as follows:

The Woman Eileen Atkins
The Man Michael Gambon

Director Matthew Warchus
Designer Mark Thompson
Lighting Designer Hugh Vanstone
Composer Gary Yershon
Sound Mic Pool
Assistant Director David Hunt
Company voice work Andrew Wade and Lyn Darnley
Production Manager Chris de Wilde
Costume Supervisor Charlotte Bird
Architectural Consultant Justin Bere of Bere Architects

Stage Manager Michael Budmani
Deputy Stage Manager Lynda Snowden
Assistant Stage Manager Anna Hill

The Man Bitter.

It's all so bitter.

The curl of my lip is bitter.

Time, things, the inanimate objects I've stacked up around me, all of which have outlived their purpose, all of which are bitter.

There's nothing to be said for objects.

My friend Yuri has a Japanese girlfriend.

Totally flat-chested.

He's sixty-eight with a three-ounce prostate, she's forty and flat-chested.

It's all so bitter. The night is bitter.

Night. No love, no closeness, drifting in and out of sleep . . .

Jean told me someone or other had written a beautiful piece on insomnia. Arsehole. Last night I woke up at five needing to shit. It's all his fault. He vetoed my All Bran. Consequently, I have to shit at five o'clock in the morning. Stupid idiot's completely sabotaged my rhythms.

What good's it to me if someone or other writes a piece about insomnia!

Yuri, now he sleeps. He's always been able to sleep.

When I can't sleep I think of Yuri, fast asleep after parsimoniously depositing a little semen in his Japanese piggy bank.

Sleeping with women is bitter.

I can't stay in bed with a woman. With certain exceptions. The black girl at the Plaza, for example.

There was some sort of contact with the black girl, it more or less worked.

I

Not the sex, but the closeness, the rub of the flesh.

The more elementary the woman, the more comfortable I feel in bed. The cruder she is. The less she interests me in life, the better I feel in bed.

Animals rubbing together, nothing else is left.

The basic question is, wouldn't I in fact be better off sleeping with an animal?

Sex is bitter.

Bitter, always has been.

No question of a biography.

Absolutely – absolutely no question of a biography after I'm dead. That's what I have to say to that lawyer.

The biography of a writer, absolutely ridiculous.

Who knows the first thing about anybody's life?

Who can say anything remotely coherent about anybody else's life?

Who can say anything remotely coherent about life in general?

Did I write what I wanted to write? No, never.

I wrote what I was capable of writing, not what I wanted to.

All you ever do is what you're capable of.

How can your complete works, your contribution added to the world – and by the way, all the great laws of nature work on the principle of subtraction – how can your complete works be anything more than a mishmash of approximations, of constantly shifting boundaries?

Isn't the end result inevitable failure?

Only anonymous writing can hope to avoid failure.

All those idiots discussing their intentions.

All those idiots shovelling out opinions, not one of them who'll admit the whole thing's slipped away, the material's uncontrollable, I can't remember the original idea and all that's left is what came limping into port.

All those poor buggers assessing their contribution to the world with furrowed brow, the great providers of

3

opinions who turn up on the books programmes.

And you're not one of them, I suppose?

No.

What do you mean, no?

No. I've never appeared on a books programme.

Never gone near a books programme.

Only because you're a snob, old boy. You've done enough other things.

Lectures, you've given. Interviews, God knows how many!

Innumerable functions in your honour.

And as for the knitted brow, no need to worry.

Yours certainly is.

Now, this minute, your brow is furrowed.

Maurice Negear is crazy about his daughter.

She came forty-seventh out of eighty-three in the Yvelines Challenge Cup.

She's a big girl. I thought jockeys were supposed to be midgets.

The Yvelines Challenge Cup . . .

What should I do? How should I proceed?

What should I do –

See him?

Follow Jean's advice and just turn up?

Have a coffee in town as if nothing's happened? Talk about the weather?

If she says he's fifty-one, he's probably twice that.

On the other hand, I can't go on ignoring him, that would definitely be a mistake.

I mean, for Christ's sake, a father has a right to object to his daughter marrying a man with one foot in the grave!

Jean says he's very nice, quite interesting even, except for his droning voice.

A droning voice and our family's been stentorian for generations.

You can't have a son-in-law with a droning voice.

Sooner or later a droning voice will provoke you to the worst excesses.

Oh, Nathalie, why couldn't you have been mad on horses like Maurice's daughter? You could have brought me back some nice sporty type.

Some nice boy, pink from forest breezes, whom I could have moulded.

Moulded in what way?

Moulded in every way. Into whatever makes a good son-in-law.

But how can you mould a fifty-one year old, who's pushing seventy?

With a droning voice.

Jean was wrong to tell me he had a droning voice.

That was the final blow.

Have a coffee in town, as if nothing's happened?

How can we pretend nothing's happened? Anyway, I never have coffee in town. The whole idea's a non-starter.

What should I do? Yet again, no idea.

The Captain of a Lost Ship.

The Woman There's always a photograph to look at.

A photograph to keep you company during the trip.

. . . In a tram in Prague in . . . 1964, there's a man sitting by the window. Looking out.

He has a high forehead, his eyes are sad, he's sixty –

He's holding his hand in front of his mouth in an attitude of contemplation which conceals half his face.

He's looking out.

Outside, there's a man standing on the pavement, with his hands in his pockets, watching the tram go by.

In the positions in which they find themselves, you could imagine that the two men were looking at each other. In fact, the two men are unaware of one another.

This encounter has no effect on either of them.

They don't even see each other.

What is it they're both looking at? The familiar course of time.

That's all they're looking at, time taking its familiar course.

If what happens happens purely by chance, there'd be no reason to dwell on this image.

There'd be no reason to dwell on anything.

My friend Serge is dead.

The world I'm looking at is a world in which my friend Serge no longer exists.

In his room at the hospital, in a drawer, there was a photograph of his mother.

A passport photo.

He took his mother with him for protection.

He was seventy-six. A man who'd been in positions of authority all his life, a grandfather himself, a man who you could say was more of a man than most, and he'd brought his mother with him, to keep in a drawer in his bedside table.

I ought to do it.

But I don't dare.

What's it matter anyhow?

And yet it does matter.

Suppose I summon up the courage to approach him between now and the time we arrive, well, I can't just sit here in silence and, without drawing attention to this coincidence in some way or another, start reading *The Unexpected Man*.

If I take *The Unexpected Man* out of my handbag, I'll have to lean towards him and say, excuse me, Mr Parsky, it just so happens I'm in the middle of reading *The Unexpected Man*, naturally I wouldn't be so insensitive as to read it in front of you –

He'll acknowledge me politely with a little smile.

And any conversation will be impossible, because that's the stupidest thing you could say.

The Man On the bridge the sailors run in all directions, some of them shouting the captain knows, others insisting the captain doesn't know, I go back to my cabin, the little Chinaman is there, pick up the rattle, I tell him, come on, little Chinaman, spin the rattle, assault my eardrums . . .

I shan't write any more.

The Captain will be my last.

Yuri must be in Buenos Aires by now.

Gone off with his Japanese on an Antarctic cruise. That's right.

It's the sort of trip you make when you've been round the world thirty-six times, you're in the twilight of your life, and what's left to you? Penguins.

Neurotics are the cream of humanity.

A droning voice.

No. No.

Mrs Cerda gets more and more cantankerous.

Jean says to me everyone else has a normal secretary and you have to have Mrs Cerda.

I have Mrs Cerda because, my boy, Mrs Cerda has been my secretary for twenty years. Which makes her absolutely irreplaceable. Yes, you have Mrs Cerda, who has her period thirty days in the month and doesn't even know how to switch on the computer.

Good! Good for her! It was stupid, buying that computer. We were fine. What did we need with a computer?

With the face and figure she's got, how could you be pleasant? She's bound to have complexes, poor woman.

All right, so she has complexes, she's not the first woman to be born ugly.

The curl of my lip is bitter.

Has it turned bitter because I'm bitter?

Or have I turned bitter through brooding on this physiological bitterness?

The feeling of getting old is bitter.

Yes. Shrivelling up is bitter.

I wasn't a bitter writer. No. No, I never wrote with bitterness.

I definitely shan't write any more.

The Captain of a Lost Ship will be my last.

The Captain of a Lost Ship, a clean book, straight up and down, the man I still hope to become.

The Woman My friend Serge didn't like your books.

It was our only quarrel.

He didn't like your short sentences, your repetitions.

He blamed you for your world view.

Negative, he used to say.

No, not at all negative.

I've never thought you were negative, Mr Parsky, quite the contrary.

All the same, what a coincidence, what a coincidence to find you sitting in front of me, in this compartment . . .

Serge, who didn't like your books and didn't like what he saw of you behind your books, said that your great stroke of luck was to have known how to make yourself lovable to me.

He said that whenever he read you, he was searching for that invisible quality which made me love you.

In the same way, I, not that I'd ever tell you this, I listened over and over again to that piece by Orlando Gibbons you're always talking about.

What attracted me towards you in the first place was your – I was going to say your love but that's not the word, no, that's not the word at all – your nearness to music, your 'bond' with music, as if the key or the lack of key to everything was to be found there.

As if music was the thing in the world most lacking from the world.

And that's what you were searching for, since you wanted no truck with eternity as such.

My desires have always outstripped whatever actually happened.

Nothing ever lives up to desire. No.

And you see I can't understand why it is we're capable of desiring so much when in the end we feel so little.

Why is desire so extravagant compared to what actually happens?

You talked about this, Mr Parsky, in *A Passer-By Like Any Other*, where you're troubled about God and afraid that just like the things you have experienced, God himself might not live up to your desire –

Let's come down to earth, dear, pretentious Mr Parsky, would you live up to my desire?

You with your highly polished shoes, your aristocratic fingernails, your mid-century elegance.

On the other hand, could I fetch out *The Unexpected Man* and not say a word?

Read without raising my eyes, occasionally looking out of the window, as if gripped by a fleeting thought . . .

I've spent my life with you, Mr Parsky.

That's to say, I've spent a few recent years of my life with you.

Which, all the same, means I've spent my life with you, because to arrive as close to you as I feel I have, I first had to reach the age I am and experience everything in the way I've experienced and understood it.

To be able to follow you down your road to what looks like excess, I've had to practise all my life.

This is what I think.

You manufacture yourself, you shape the raw material, then you lay it open to the unexpected.

For a long time I've been attracted by people who don't care for the world and are tormented by non-stop suffering.

It seemed to me that the desperate were the only profound, the only really attractive people.

Fundamentally, if I'm honest, I thought them superior.

For a long time I felt myself to be less interesting, not to say less admirable, because I loved life.

Whereas you, you claim not to love anything, you complain about everything, but in your rage, in your vitriolic energy, I see life itself.

And, not wishing to infuriate you, I also see joy.

I talk to you secretly. Secretly, I tell you everything I can never tell you.

How to approach you, you in the twilight of your life, I in mine, and say something appropriate to our age?

Read without saying a word.

Are you even going to notice?

Have you even looked my way?

Since our journey began, have you raised your eyes in my direction one single time?

When I'm not facing towards you, I feel as if you're watching me, but when I decide to connect with you silently, you're somewhere else.

The Man Detested the way Elie spoke to me about *The Unexpected Man*.

Detested it so much, I can't bear to see him again.

I'm repeating myself. So?

I'm repeating myself. Yes. Well, of course, I'm repeating myself.

That's what I do. What else is there to do?

In fact, little Elie, you didn't even use the phrase 'repeat yourself'. If you'd said 'you're repeating yourself', I would have sensed some small degree of pleasant familiarity in the 'you're repeating yourself', I would have discerned the affection, the affectionate bluntness of a friend. What you did say, so embarrassed you were squirming around like a woman, was it's very like, it's very like things you've written before. Things I've written before which you adored, Elie Breitling!

Except now, there's been a change of idol.

What you adored, you adored when it was new, 'undissected', on the fringes of fashion.

Not original, but new.

I emphasize new, and not original. Two diametrically opposed concepts.

When it comes to it, you've never had the patience, the discreet patience for unconditional love.

The craze for novelty.

Is it what are you actually saying? No. It's what are you saying that's new?

What's new?

Who's your new idol, little Elie?

Of course, I could always find out by reading your column . . . it's ages since I gave up reading your column.

Did I ever read it? Even when you were the pioneer of my ultra-novelty, acclaiming in your articles all my worst qualities.

Bitter.

Could I possibly have turned bitter?

No.

The Woman You're a man with whom I'd like to have discussed certain things.

In fact, people with whom you'd like to discuss things are not all that thick on the ground.

I, who was so biased in favour of men, finished up by turning my back on their friendships.

My best friends, my few rare and singular friends, are women.

That women would turn out to be better friends to me than men is a development I could never have predicted.

Apart from my friend Serge, who's now dead, I had another friend.

His name was Georges.

Georges was slightly in love with me.

In that charming way men have of being slightly in love with you, without expecting anything. I was married.

And our friendship contained a hint of mischief, a . . . how shall I put it, a knowing closeness.

I laughed a great deal with Georges, Mr Parsky. You know how it is when you can laugh. By the way, I've often laughed in your company.

One day, Georges arrived with a woman.

He thought it acceptable to introduce a woman into our relationship. He committed the solecism of comparing us.

I am not a woman, Mr Parsky, who invites comparisons.

Nor am I a woman to be weighed against anyone or anything.

Sixteen years of friendship and he still hadn't grasped that.

Worse, he confided in me.

Worse still, he asked my advice.

Sixteen years of pleasantly double-edged friendship collapsed in three sentences.

The poor man didn't even realize – of course, when I say the poor man I'm speaking purely from my point of view – because he was, and this was what was most intolerable: happy.

Happy, Mr Parsky.

I was very civilized about it.

To have so often been civilized about things is perhaps where I've gone wrong in life.

Georges married this woman – she was one of his patients, Georges is a dentist – and he had a child.

We used to have lunch occasionally.

We both went on pretending we were still intimates.

To start with, Georges kept his end up.

Our conversations, although meatless, because the meat of a conversation obviously doesn't lie in what's actually

said, still retained the glow of our old conversations.

And then, feeling free, God knows why, as time went on, Georges began to talk to me about his son.

A certain Eric.

How Georges could have called his son Eric remains a mystery to me.

We never talked about my children – I have two – although he no doubt remembered I was a mother myself.

Among parents you expect a bit of mutual unbosoming, don't you?

Eric was a treasure, Mr Parsky. A little treasure.

You put him to bed. Bam, he was asleep.

You woke him up. He started gurgling.

His little hands were so strong. His little arms were so loving. Eric sang all day long. The father was happy, the child was secure, what could be more natural?

One day, Georges said to me quite seriously, with tears in his eyes, when I take him out in his push-chair, I'm sorry for the people who walk past without smiling at him.

Out of George's mouth, the word 'push-chair'!

The least domesticated of men. Or so I thought.

A man I'd known as outrageous and insolent, reduced to shreds, liquefied by paternity.

And who, with no memory of himself or me, sat there boasting of his liquefaction.

One evening, and I'm finally getting to what I wanted to tell you in the first place, we went to listen to some Brahms sonatas. It was a long time since we'd spent an evening together.

After the concert, he took me to a Thai restaurant I particularly liked and after dinner we had a drink at the Crillon bar.

How can I explain this to you? The whole evening had gone by under some star unshackled from time. Not a word about Eric, or push-chairs, not a word about mar-

ried patients, just a couple of could-be lovers, as in the past, arm-in-arm, laughing, faintly disreputable.

He took me back to my house. He walked me.

He walked me because he didn't have his car.

As we walked, I felt able to flirt quite freely as before and the air was sweet.

In front of my door, where, in earlier days, we would linger, sometimes for hours, I suddenly had the feeling he was in a hurry . . .

We said goodnight with an impersonal kiss and I watched him running, Mr Parsky, running, racing to look for a taxi, running desperately back to his little family, back to his own, running like a man who'd finally snapped his chains –

The Man I don't see why I shouldn't go back on Ex-Lax.

I was happy with Ex-Lax.

Jean says it's dangerous. What is he, a doctor? When all's said and done, I don't see why I should listen to my son, who isn't a doctor and who, not content with being round-shouldered, smokes.

Ex-Lax suited me.

It was a comfortable way to download.

Curious word, download. We never said download in my day.

Ex-Lax was a success.

Full stop.

Can never remember the name of that quasi-son-in-law. Henri? Gérard? – Rémy?

Rémy Sledz.

Sledz. Yes.

'Mr Sledz, you're planning to live with my daughter –'

Don't be stupid, they've been living together for months.

'Mr Sledz, you're planning to –' ugh, I refuse to utter the verb 'marry', the verb 'marry' is not in my repertoire –

'Mr Sledz, I imagine you must appreciate a father's

concerns –' If he answers, of course, I keep putting myself in your shoes, I'll strangle him with my bare hands.

Stay cool. Don't get involved.

Is it right for me to get involved in her life?

What is it that counts? The long run? Or the moment? What is it that's really of value?

In the train carrying him from Paris to Frankfurt, Paul Parsky still has no idea of the value of time.

I refuse to give in.

No surrender.

The Woman You once said in an interview that as a writer you had no opinions and that you had no intention of saying anything whatsoever on any given subject, and that you greatly admired philosophers, or great mathematicians, anyone from the world of ideas, and that you yourself had done nothing but notice certain things and interpret what you'd noticed, but that never, never in a million years, had your writing shown any tendency or inclination to enter the world of ideas.

You said in this interview that ideas about the world were strictly speaking of no value in the practice of literature.

Sheer hypocrisy.

I've never found anything in any of your books which doesn't express in a completely personal way your view of the world.

Even your energy is a view of the world.

Your allergy to nuance is a view of the world.

Your disinclination to do the sensible thing is a view of the world.

Reading your interview, I finally grasped something unexpected: your fear of being understood, Mr Parsky.

You cover your tracks, you personally invent protective misunderstandings, because you're haunted by the fear of being understood.

Pursued, yes.

Understood, no.

A judicious helping of impenetrability is how you avert this great misfortune and preserve your prestige intact.

In *The Unexpected Man* which is in my handbag, your hero, your alter ego, claims he only wanted to be someone in order to be able to abdicate.

When are you, my dear writer, planning to abdicate?

I see no signs of abdication anywhere.

Not in your flirtatious isolation, and not in those immoderately offhand comments you squeeze out about yourself.

And certainly not in your writing.

In *The Unexpected Man* which I have in my handbag, you don't for one second give up any of the illusions of the human race.

If ever a man was far from giving them up, it's you, my poor old thing.

Absurd to feel intimidated by you.

Really ridiculous.

'Mr Parsky, chance, wonderful chance – or rather, chance, quite simply – chance has decreed that I should meet you on this train; I can't resist telling you . . .'

And what are you going to tell him?

How will you fight your way back up from that kind of affectation?

'Mr Parsky, I'm prepared to risk any kind of adventure with you.'

Just to see his face.

If he laughs, if he genuinely laughs, he's the man I think he is.

Come on, Martha, life is short.

And what if he doesn't laugh?

If he doesn't laugh, he's not the man you think he is, so you'll wind down the window and throw out *The Unexpected Man*.

And you'll be so ashamed, you'll throw yourself out after it.

And what if he genuinely does laugh?

If he genuinely does laugh . . .

This is torture! . . .

The Man Can never sleep on a train.

Hard enough in bed, let alone on a train.

Strange this woman never reads anything.

A woman who doesn't read anything the whole journey.

Not even a spot of *Marie Claire*.

Perhaps I should write for the theatre?

No, no, no . . . God, no!

How could it even cross my mind!

Something must have come loose in my brain.

Besides, in the theatre, the only thing I can stand is boulevard comedy.

Basically.

At a boulevard comedy, the audience laughs like normal people.

They don't laugh in that deathly way you hear these days in the palaces of culture.

Laughter congratulating itself for being intelligent enough to know why it's being laughed.

A little *in* laugh in several stages.

The way Elie Breitling laughed during *Measure for Measure*.

That's right. That's the way Elie laughs these days.

It's something new. He never used to laugh like that. No, no, there was a time, when Elie was in a crowd, he laughed like a normal person.

A time when Elie would have talked to me about *The Unexpected Man* in his kitchen at three o'clock in the morning in front of his fifteenth Fernet Branca and I would have hung on every word.

Is there today one single person in the whole world, in

the whole world, who might know how to read that book?

The Woman I'm not on good terms with Nadine, Serge's wife.

Serge used to have adventures, and she knew I knew.

She thought I condoned them.

It's a pity our relationship disintegrated.

Nadine always respected my friendship with Serge.

She's an intelligent woman.

Things deteriorated when Serge started to have adventures.

Adventures – may be something of an exaggeration. Anyway.

As she got older, Nadine blew up like a balloon. And when a woman blows up like a balloon, a man begins to look elsewhere.

I'm talking to you about Serge, Mr Parsky, because Serge was one of your characters.

He didn't like you, but if they were to read you, would your characters like you?

Let's imagine Strattmer reading *The Unexpected Man*.

I'd say he'd get impatient after about two pages.

Like Strattmer, Serge was an insomniac.

One night, when he couldn't sleep and he was tossing and turning in his bed, he tried to calm himself by thinking about Auschwitz.

He conjured up the discomfort of the mattresses, the stench of the latrines, the lack of space, here you are, he said to himself, in your soft bed with your clean sheets, you don't have some neighbour's stinking feet in your mouth, you don't have to get up and carry away that disgusting bucket: so go to sleep!

Go to sleep, Serge old chap!

Just at the moment he was about to fall asleep, he said to himself, wait a minute! An idea which ought to haunt

you, and give you no peace, and you're using it as a
soporific!

A horror which you did not experience, and you're
turning it into a tranquillizer?!

He wanted to write something about this confusion. He
got up to look for some paper.

Couldn't find any.

I woke Nadine up, he told me, she, let's be fair, has no
need to think about Auschwitz to get off to sleep, and I
said how can it be possible, how can it be possible I said,
this is what Serge told me, and you can see how calm I
am, I'm saying this very calmly, how can it be possible that
there is not one piece of paper in this house?

I can't bear people who sleep.

How can people sleep? How can they sleep well?

If I may say so, Martha – Serge was seventeen years
older than me and we always maintained a certain formal-
ity – if I may say so, Martha, I know you're a poor sleeper
and that is the cornerstone of our friendship. Nadine
sleeps. It's her latest enthusiasm. She's a sleeper.

She used to be a woman you could rely on for a conversation any time of the night.

One day, I shall publish my theory about sleepers.

We were having lunch that day – as a hypochondriac,
Serge left you standing – and I said to him, you're looking
bonny. What do you mean, I'm looking bonny! I haven't
slept a wink all night and I'm looking bonny?! Perhaps it's
a circulation problem?!

He got up and went to check his complexion in the gents!

Before he died, he said to me, I don't want a single word
spoken at my funeral.

Be so good as to be there to check.

As for music, I'd be happy with Schumann, but I
wouldn't want to seem too romantic.

Be honest, Mr Parsky, Serge is one of your characters,
isn't he?

Mr Parsky, I'm afraid I miss my friend Serge terribly.

The Man To think, all those years, and I knew nothing about Debussy.

Thirty years without hearing a note of Debussy.

I got through 'Clair de Lune' all right the day before yesterday.

For the teacher to suggest 'La Cathédrale engloutie', he must have been impressed by the progress I've made.

Good idea to take up the piano again.

There's been a maturing . . . a mental leap forward . . .

How could Nathalie have said to me that Yuri plays better than I do?

Has she no ear?

Well, of course it's true I don't attempt the same pieces as Mr Yuri Kogloff. I don't attempt Scriabin, I don't play 'L'Ile joyeuse'.

I'm too fond of music.

He even plays 'Scarbo'.

It's all wrong, the tempo's shot to hell, bum notes from beginning to end.

He plays like an old Jewish refugee in a bar.

And my own daughter is taken in.

She tells me I don't know how to use the pedal.

She's right.

In any case, I use it less and less.

Pieces which require the pedal are few and far between.

Even Schubert. Even with Schubert, I manage that 'Impromptu' very well without bothering with the pedal.

I play it very efficiently. All right, in an ideal world, you'd use the pedal, if you knew how to. But without the pedal, it's not bad at all, in fact it's rather good.

Yuri knows all about the pedal.

When Yuri sits down at the piano, his Japanese is ecstatic.

Yuri will play in front of anyone.

He has no shame.

The more he waters it down, the better his Japanese likes it.

It's true I'm ready to attempt 'La Cathédrale engloutie'.

There are two reasons behind my progress.

First, I'm getting better and better at sight-reading. Thanks to Bach, I've got used to a strong, quick left hand, which compels you to anticipate.

And secondly, I've succeeded in hearing myself.

Easy enough to hear other people play. It's hearing oneself, that's what's difficult.

I have to ask my teacher to let me work on some of the 'Waldszenen'.

I've always had a feeling for Schumann. Now that I've matured.

'Vogel als Prophet', that's what I must play. That'll be my next piece.

If I were a painter, I'd draw this woman's face.

It's a disturbing face. Cold . . . no, disturbingly indifferent.

A woman who might fire the imagination.

The Woman When Serge said to me before he died that he wanted Schumann at his funeral, but that he was afraid of seeming too romantic, I laughed.

Of course I laughed. But he said, how can you laugh?

Don't you remember when you had your hip operation and were convinced you'd never come round from the anaesthetic, you said to me, if I die, whatever you do don't let them put my age in *le Figaro*!

Which of us is the more frivolous?

Frivolous beyond the grave, we are.

How to accept that somebody we loved is dead.

How to accept that the world contains one less person to love us . . .

My parents are gone.

A husband I loved, gone.

So many friends, dead.

Serge, dead.

How to accept never being in control of time or loneliness.

It was a good idea to have my hair done before I left.

Last time she made it too blonde, but this time she's done it well.

And I was right to wear my yellow suit. I needn't have worried I'd be cold in it and it gives me an air of mystery.

If that idiotic writer deigned to glance over in my direction, he would see me at my best.

At least that's some satisfaction.

Do you really think man hasn't changed since the stone age?

I'm dying to ask you the question. Do you really think, as you maintain the whole way through *The Unexpected Man*, that man's knowledge is the only thing about him that's evolved?

It's not your invention, the theory that knowledge makes no difference.

Of course it isn't, but you develop it with such bitterness.

Your outlook is so bitter.

If I insist on talking to you – even though it's in secret – about Serge, it's because in my mind there are so many ways the two of you are connected.

One day I called him, stupidly excited about the fall of the Berlin Wall. Fine, he said, yes, so what? Its coming down won't improve the behaviour of mankind.

– Deep down I wonder if there wasn't a touch of jealousy in his antipathy towards you; it must have annoyed him that I kept unearthing his character and his thoughts in your books. Another time we were talking about Tiananmen Square and he said I couldn't care less about the Chinese students, I still prefer the Iranians.

I prefer whirling dervishes to human rights.

Serge, always excessive, like Strattmer, and like you.

Not an ounce of self-restraint.

An attractiveness essentially based on character flaws.

I was so low when I packed last night!

Do men ever suffer that kind of low?

Still felt sad this morning.

Sad at the station.

A woman who travels from Paris to Frankfurt with nothing else to read but *The Unexpected Man* is a deeply depressed woman.

One day I'd like someone to explain to me why sadness always catches you by surprise, when everything seems under control.

What the hell, I'm fetching out the book.

I'm fetching out the book. I'll place myself so he can see me. He can't not react. He can't watch me embarking on an intimate relationship with him six feet away without revealing himself. What are you going to do in Frankfurt?

The Book Fair? No. First of all, I don't think it's the time of year, and a writer with your nature, flirtatiously antisocial, doesn't turn up at the Book Fair.

So what can you be doing there?

Oh, God, make him speak to me.

The Man What's she going to do in Frankfurt?

Visit a relative? Work?

No, she has a lover in the petrochemical industry.

This woman doesn't have a husband, she has a lover. In the petrochemical industry. Excellent.

Unless she's quite simply German.

On her way home.

She's not German. No.

Why? Why isn't she German?

At any rate, if she's German, she's not from Frankfurt. Anyway, no, she isn't a German. Germans don't look out

of the window like that. She's a woman who's going somewhere. Not a woman who's coming back.

Should I approach her?

What would I say?

What's it matter if she's German or what she is? But, yes, the worm is in the bud, I have to know.

I'll approach her.

He speaks to her.

>Please excuse me, do you think we might open the window a bit?

The Woman Yes, it is quite warm. By all means.

You answered my prayer!

Such a trivial prayer and you answered it!

Listened to a couple of insignificant words which could have no possible bearing on the higher course of time and tide.

Oh, God, have I ever once prayed to you without asking for a favour?

Maybe I ought not to get to know you, Mr Parsky.

Suppose I don't like you, why take the risk of no longer being able to love anything about you?

I'm told there isn't necessarily an intimate link between a man and his work.

How can that be possible?

I should have . . . I should have said something else instead of smiling like a fool. I was caught on the hop.

Now he's sunk back, deep in his thoughts.

What a dimwit.

After all, I have a perfect right to break the silence as well.

Even if I only do it once.

But what would I say?

Something absolutely banal would be most appropriate, least heavy.

Whatever else happens, I don't want to make him think I'm jumping feet first into a conversation.

What leads on from the window? . . .

The Man French. I knew it.

French. An affecting voice.

A hint of strangeness.

Her lover's a conductor. Why not?

He's about to conduct 'Verklärte Nacht'.

Afterwards you'll spend the night in Wiesbaden.

Friday you'll be in Mainz, where you'll buy a painting which strongly resembles you, by some minor *cinquecento* master.

The painting is called *The Portrait and Dream of Giovanna Alviste*.

In it you're leaning forward slightly, three-quarters in shadow, looking out of a window at a blurred landscape with a bridge.

Both of you stopped dead in front of the painting in the antique shop. Because there on the canvas, melancholy in the moonlight, are your unmistakable features, your very particular eyes, gazing out in a distinctively watchful and supercilious way.

You buy the painting. No, not you, the conductor buys the painting.

He tells you he's going to keep it in his bedroom so he can contemplate you every day with complete impunity.

You laugh.

You laugh and try to remember who you were when you were *Giovanna Alviste*.

A splinter of life among so many others, a tiny pinprick in time, amid so much pointless loneliness, so many heaped-up splinters, scraps of dead wood scattered across our paths . . .

Bitter.

Why did I pay for Mrs Cerda to go to Biarritz?

What could have prompted such generosity?

Her great bollocks of a son was there. She was hoping to avert some cock-up by offering him a scooter.

I've always regretted my moments of virtue.

All those 'noble' gestures, after the event I've always discovered some tainted reason for having made them.

Mrs Cerda's been a complete wreck since the collapse of Communism.

The only life Mrs Cerda knew was standing firm against the reds.

In a case like that, what's the use of Biarritz?

Nathalie told me that . . . what's his name again . . .?

Sledz. Sledz adored *A Passer-By Like Any Other*.

People keep talking to me about books I wrote thirty years ago!

I can't even remember what it was about. Seriously, I've no idea.

He liked *A Passer-By Like Any Other*, so did everybody else, great, obviously he read it a couple of weeks ago, as far as he's concerned it's the present, Paul Parsky in the present, whereas for me it's a book written by somebody quite other.

There's some misunderstanding about time.

What we produce stagnates. Ossifies. Only plays an active part in other people's minds.

In time what a man produces becomes what's furthest from him.

To start with, what's he doing reading *A Passer-By Like Any Other*? Instead of, let's say, *The Remark*, which is far better. Not to mention *The Unexpected Man*.

Which actually I would have disapproved of, because it's too recent.

All in all, I prefer it that he's dug up the *Passer-By*, rather than plunging into *The Unexpected Man*.

Plunging into *The Unexpected Man* before he'd met me would have been the worst, the worst sort of blunder.

. . . 'Mr Sledz, my trip to Frankfurt has given me a chance to reassess our situation . . .'

What do you mean, *our*? He couldn't care less about *my* situation.

That's exactly what I have against him! He has no consideration for me!

The Woman I like travelling.

As soon as I set foot in Frankfurt, I shall be another person: the one who arrives is always another person.

And so it is that one progresses, from one person to another, until it's all over.

Mr Parsky, you rested your eyes on me in a certain way, there was a question mark in your bright eyes.

For a brief instant in your life, possibly imperceptible even to yourself, I'm sure I had some effect on you.

What was your question?

Whatever it is, the answer's yes.

Yes, it's me.

I'm the one who, secretly, one day, will make off with your world, I'm the one, I'll make off with your light, your face, your happy hours or sad, the days and nights your name is on, the whole of time to ashes.

I'm the one. The one who loved you, who coloured you according to my inclinations, the one who studied every subject under your perpetual catechism, I shall abolish you, I shall make off with you when my time is up and nothing will remain of you or of anything else.

That was my answer when you rested your eyes on me and spoke to me of fresh air.

I have a brother, who lives in Paris. Older than me.

We keep on talking about other people, because we're made up of other people, don't you agree?

As a writer, you know that better than anyone.

My brother lives in Paris, in a handsome apartment building in the 17th *arrondissement*.

The hallway in his building is paved with white, beige and black flagstones.

He's been living in his building for twenty-five years, and for twenty-five years, every day that God sends, my brother has only stepped on the light-coloured flagstones, alternating, according to a very precise and never varying formula, between white and beige.

Never, in twenty-five years, has he stepped on a black flagstone.

And anybody with him is forbidden to step on the black flagstones which are somehow more tempting than the others.

When he inadvertently passes the concierge, on whom he's never dared impose his ban, he closes his eyes so as not to witness her sacrilege.

He told me he was petitioning the Residents' Association to have her replaced because, and I quote, she was an irresponsible woman who, in defiance of all common sense, was pulverizing the chessboard.

My brother is convinced that the world order depends on the flawlessness of his passage.

A world order which comprises all possible journeys, including, Mr Parsky, ours in this Paris to Frankfurt train.

And if, in turn, I make so bold as to address you, it will be because, in the great labyrinth of life, my brother or I, according to the rules, have happened to stand on the correct stone.

Right. That's enough philosophizing.

We're already beyond Strasbourg. Time for action.

Some banal phrase. No.

I'm fetching out the book.

She fetches The Unexpected Man *out of her handbag.*

The funniest thing would be if he didn't even notice.

Come on, Martha, employ a little cunning in the way you read.

Discreet but unmistakably strong on presence.

My heart is beating.

I'm twelve years old – What a trip!

The Man How many times in my youth did I think, ah, old age! – happiness – calm – no more pretence!

Buffoon!

Ah, old age! Now what's it look like?

An old boy with a rancorous expression. The kind of man who takes umbrage when his old friend Breitling utters the ghost of a reservation.

No, no. No, it wasn't the ghost of a reservation.

Let's not understate it.

And if we didn't care what people said to us, why would we struggle on with a pursuit which is at the mercy of outside opinion?

An old man in thrall to the judgments of his contemporaries, condemned, whatever he may say, to try to put a good face on it.

But for whose benefit? For whose benefit?

She's reading.

. . . She's reading *The Unexpected Man*! . . .

Extraordinary . . .

Where's she got to?

Page . . . page . . . 120? . . .

Extraordinary . . .

120 . . . Strattmer's in hospital.

He's already met Reuvens. She must have read the chapter about the counting mania. Or else she's in the middle of it.

No, she's not laughing, she must have finished reading it. Unless she's in the middle of it and she doesn't think it's funny. No, no.

This woman would be laughing. I'm sure of it. She must have gone past it.

You couldn't read about the counting mania without at least smiling.

She is smiling! She's smiling! She's in the middle of it!

Strattmer meets Reuvens who talks to him about his counting mania, which Strattmer also suffers from – one of many.

Don't stare at her so insistently. You'll break her concentration.

Extraordinary –

She doesn't know who I am, no. No, of course not.

She wouldn't just be innocently reading like that. She doesn't know who I am.

Why didn't she start reading it when we set off?

Lack of interest. No. Just look at her expression.

A good face on it for whose benefit? For whose benefit, my old Parsky? Why, for hers, for your unforeseen travelling companion, this silent woman sent to you by fate, the focus of your beseeching gaze.

She's reading *The Unexpected Man*.

It's really too much.

I knew she was an interesting woman.

Shall I remain anonymous?

Why wasn't she reading it when we set off?

Because she had things to think about.

In Frankfurt, she's going to break up with the conductor.

She was thinking about methods of breaking up.

About turns of phrase to use when breaking up. In their relationship they've always weighed their words.

She's going to break up with the conductor and *The Unexpected Man* is the book she's chosen as witness to this moment.

Remain anonymous? Absolutely.

But aren't I likely to feel some sort of bitterness?

57

As usual. What's the point of these scruples?

Which will probably deprive me of a simple pleasure.

Anyway, it's not so much scruples, as you hasten to flatter yourself, it's more like discretion, not to say cowardice.

Isn't the benefit I might derive from this strange occurrence, by simply remembering it and passing it on to others, enough?

Not enough.

I have to reveal myself.

But maybe in two stages.

The Woman '. . . As far as my daughter's concerned, Strattmer, I consider myself unclean. I've always been afraid of infecting her. I was tidying away some fish scraps in the kitchen, when I spotted a slice of lime. I licked it; I like the taste, it reminds me of Mexico. I put it back on the table. I said to myself, you can't leave it there, contaminated, where anyone could pick it up. You can't throw it away, it cost you one franc seventy-five, it's a lime, they're hard to come by. So I bit into it and chewed it until it was ready to be thrown away. During these five minutes of oral acidity, I performed the electrified dance imposed on me by my limbs and took the opportunity to tot up the number of cupboard handles in the room, items which curiously enough I had never previously counted.'

How strange that I was telling you about my brother.

This counting mania is exactly what my brother suffers from.

My brother is the victim of counting mania and, to that extent, he's also part of your universe.

Oh, my God, what you write about is so familiar to me!

And you're so far away.

I've made a mistake.

You're not going to speak to me.

There was a time, Mr Parsky, when I had no need to get embroiled in books and handbags and failures of nerve . . .

I was beautiful and that spoke for me.

He's seen me.

He's watching me, he's seen the book.

Here we go.

I didn't wear my yellow suit for nothing.

I didn't get into this compartment for nothing.

Nothing's for nothing.

I'll count to twenty and then I'll say . . .

What will you say, Martha?

I'll say . . .

Think of the sentence and then count.

The Man A famous author goes on a journey and sits opposite an unknown woman who's reading his latest book.

Good subject for a short story.

Bit old-fashioned.

Could have been written by . . . by whom?

Stefan Zweig. Yes . . . Or Manuel Torga – Yes.

The man's intimidated.

A man who prides himself on having outgrown such childishness is suddenly touched by the indelicacy of the situation.

The woman's attractive.

Would he be intimidated if the woman wasn't attractive?

If the woman wasn't attractive, he would withdraw into his distaste for what's called the public, that breed never to be encountered.

Let's be honest. You've never done anything for no reason or for nobody. You don't create in a void.

You throw bottles into the sea desperately hoping for a castaway.

To produce, to add to the world is to experience the magic of possibility.

Here goes.

How would you account for the need to invent or dream up other lives?
Isn't it enough quite simply to exist, what do you think?

The Woman   I don't know what you mean by quite sim-ply to exist. There's no such thing as quite simply.

The Man   That book you're holding, it so happens I've read it as well –

The Woman   Oh, really? . . .

The Man   Do you like it?

The Woman   I'm not sure I can answer such a blunt ques-tion.
This is an author I've been close to for some time . . .

The Man   You as well.

The Woman   You as well?

The Man   For some time. Yes. What have you read?

The Woman   *A Passer-By Like Any Other* . . . A small collection of short stories, can't remember the title . . . *The Remark, The Poor Man's Footstep* . . .

The Man	Did you like *The Poor Man's Footstep*?
The Woman	Yes . . . For me, it's the most moving. What about you?
The Man	. . . I remember it as being quite a personal book.
The Woman	Yes, that's what I'd say. Personal. Inevitable. And which must have felt inevitable to the man who wrote it.
The Man	Could be. You can't always write like that.
The Woman	No. I'm sure.
The Man	You can only lay yourself naked once.
The Woman	I'm sure.
	Pause.
The Man	You don't want to talk to me about this book?
The Woman	I can't talk about it before I've finished it.
The Man	Yes, you can. I mean, the ending has no significance.
The Woman	Well . . . the book says the same thing to me as that photograph of Prague above your head . . . It's given me, yet again, a nostalgia for what's never taken place. A nostalgia for what might happen.

Does it deal with anything else?

The Man   Don't you find it irritatingly repetitious?

The Woman   Yes. But I never read without being irritated.
He's a deeply irritating writer.

The Man   He certainly is.

The Woman   You find him irritating as well?

The Man   Yes, yes, irritating. Very irritating.
Are you going to Frankfurt?

The Woman   Yes.

Pause.

The Man   He's an irritating writer and in my view a
minor writer.
You're quite wrong to interest yourself in
him.

The Woman   Irritating, yes. Minor, no.
Everything you love is irritating.

The Man   He's a selfish little busybody who's never
been able to turn a single moment into an
eternity, which is the mark of a poet, he
can't speak of death except cynically, snig-
gering like some pathetic old hag, he claims
to hate the crowd and the masses, but he's
never known how to describe man's unhap-
piness, the only sadness he can talk about is
his own, about which he is maniacally repetitious! There's a sentence he envies in an

67

elegy by Borges: 'On the other side of the door,' Borges says, 'a man made out of love, of time and of loneliness has just been weeping in Buenos Aires for everything that is.' You see, Paul Parsky has never known how to weep for everything that is.

Silence.

The Woman I think you're very unfair.
But I don't believe you mean it, since you said all that with the kind of effrontery which implies the opposite.
In *The Remark*, he sees a middle-aged woman in a metro station, a fat woman with a shawl and a heavy coat. She's crying, her face is pressed up against the grubby white tiles of the wall, right next to a poster for *Holiday on Ice*.
She has slippers on her feet, and ankle-socks pulled up over her swollen calves.
He describes her feet, her slippers, the bruised skin between her socks and her coat and through this the whole of her life, her entire life in five lines . . .
In another book, he talks about watching his grandfather out of the window as he turns the corner by the house and tiptoes away like a child, clutching the results of his medical tests.
And in *The Unexpected Man*, come to that, there's that woman who has lunch by herself every Sunday at the Blue Sea Hotel in Royan, plastered with make-up, her hair dyed, dressed in pink, ridiculed and sneered at by everybody, about whom nev-

ertheless you say . . . that she was kindness itself . . . All these things and so many others you've described, Mr Parsky, have made me weep . . .
You have no right to be bitter.
In your books there have been hundreds of moments like eternity. And if I have to prove myself worthy of whatever devil has dropped me down in this compartment, I'm forced to admit I've been madly in love with you and that in another life – since I wouldn't like to embarrass you – I would have taken off with you, on any kind of adventure . . .

He laughs.